W9-CFB-332

Makerspace Careers™

CAREERS IN
INTERACTIVE
MEDIA

JANET HARVEY

Rosen
YA™
New York

Published in 2020 by The Rosen Publishing Group, Inc.
29 East 21st Street, New York, NY 10010

First Edition

Library of Congress Cataloging-in-Publication Data

Names: Harvey, Janet, 1966– author.
Title: Careers in interactive media / Janet Harvey.
Description: First edition. | New York : Rosen Publishing, 2020. | Series: Makerspace careers | Includes bibliographical references and index.
Identifiers: LCCN 2018051630| ISBN 9781508188049 (library bound) | ISBN 9781508188032 (pbk.)
Subjects: LCSH: Interactive multimedia—Vocational guidance—Juvenile literature. | Computer games—Programming—Juvenile literature. Classification: LCC QA76.76.I59 H39 2020 | DDC 794.8/1536—dc23
LC record available at https://lccn.loc.gov/2018051630

Manufactured in China

CONTENTS

INTRODUCTION

In the realm of entertainment, interactivity is becoming a key part of what people do for fun. We use our phones to walk around the neighborhood and "catch" virtual creatures. We call up our favorite movies and shows from an online menu, sometimes just by using voice commands. And in gaming, virtual reality (VR) headsets are creating whole virtual worlds for us to immerse ourselves in and interact with.

Interactive media is an ever-growing and expanding field. The job outlook for interactive media is strong: field growth is outpacing the national average, and salaries for interactive media jobs average about $45,000. But how can you prepare yourself for the dream jobs that will be out there in ten to twenty years? In such a rapidly growing, unpredictable field, what's the best way to jump in and start building the skills of the future?

One of the most reliable ways to get hands-on experience in coding and designing for interactive media is through makerspaces and hackerspaces. Many schools and communities are creating such spaces. Joining a creative space is a great way to gain experience with equipment and resources that you might not otherwise have access to. In makerspaces and hackerspaces, you can develop skills in interactive media development and design, digital media

Pikachu / CP ???

Pokémon Go was one of the first games to use augmented reality—a technology that superimposes computer-generated images on top of the real world.

production, Arduino coding, game design, robot creation, and three-dimensional (3D) printing.

If this sounds like something out of a cyberpunk novel … well, it kind of is. From the first hackerspaces of the 1990s until today, hackerspaces have been run by loosely organized groups of "hackers" and like-minded techno-geeks with a desire to learn and a do-it-yourself (DIY) attitude. Gathering in rented studios, lofts, or warehouses, they would pool their resources and knowledge in the interest of learning and cooperation, enabling the group to access equipment and resources that the individual members might not be able to acquire on their own.

As more and more people see the value of these types of spaces, hackerspaces have been showing up in different areas of study, at universities, and even in libraries. Makerspaces, an offshoot of hackerspaces, took the same concept into fabrication.

The world of digital media also took a page from the hackerspace/makerspace book, and today you can find digital media labs that share resources, software, hardware, equipment, and work space in the spirit of sharing information in the digital age.

Today, there are 2,289 hackerspaces around the world, with 1,418 of them listed as "active," according to Hackerspaces.org. Hackerspaces continue to grow at an amazing rate. You may even have one in your own school or library. If you don't, the good news is you can probably start your own. There are plenty of resources out there to help you start your own makerspace, hackerspace, or digital media lab.

How can a hackerspace help you get the job of your dreams? Get ready to find out.

CHAPTER ONE

A BRIEF HISTORY OF HACKERSPACES

The term "hacker" originally meant "hacking" technology in ways that would make it do something it wasn't intended to do. Today, we use the term "hacking" to describe a variety of purposes and activities, from "hacking" our closet to make our morning routine more efficient, to more nefarious computer "hacks," like breaking into an internet server or stealing someone's identity. For a lot of people, the term has come to be associated with criminal activity—and because of this, the term "computer hacker" has come to have a negative connotation.

But that wasn't always the case. The original hackers were simply hardware, software, and programming enthusiasts who were interested in using digital tools and the internet in new ways to create something that didn't exist before. They would be more likely to build a robot that made you coffee in the morning than use their skills to rob a bank. Hacker culture introduced open-source

When you think of "hacker culture," you may think of anonymous sinister figures—but it really refers to any technology "hack" that makes your life better.

programming, a type of programming that anyone can use without a license. Hackers continue to push the boundaries of what code and hardware can do.

The birth of hackerspaces can be traced back to the mid-1990s, when the first hackerspace, called C-Base, was launched in Berlin in 1995. It was basically a community space where computer programmers met, worked, and shared infrastructure, trying to use new technologies in creative ways.

As time went on, the hacker movement evolved into the maker movement, as people started using technology to create physical items in the real world with digital tools, like computer numerical control (CNC) routers, 3D printers, and other fabrication tools. The maker movement continues the traditions of hacker culture by freely sharing information, plans, and techniques over the internet—and by sharing resources with makerspaces.

AN ALIEN SPACE STATION IN BERLIN

Widely recognized as the earliest hackerspace, C-Base in Berlin was founded in 1995. From its inception, the space was envisioned as a creative hub, with the creation of computer software, hardware, and data being part of a broader movement of music, design, and digital media creation.

C-Base is home to the Chaos Computer Club (CCC), Europe's largest association of hackers. Self-described as "a galactic community of life forms, independent of age, sex, race or societal orientation, which strives

This is the interior of C-Base in Berlin, Germany. C-Base is widely considered the first hackerspace.

across borders for freedom of information," the CCC advocates for the free transfer of information and supports open-source software, more transparency, and decentralization of power.

C-Base hosts musical concerts, theatrical performances, and art exhibitions, in addition to presentations and children's computer camps—even a space food design competition called Space Meal! It is also host to the Berlin Wikipedia editors group, and the space is used in cooperation with the Transmediale conference, an annual festival of digital art and culture.

Even the origin story of C-Base is a crowd-sourced history, which created the myth that C-Base was founded in the remnants of a crashed space station. According to the stories of the members of C-base, the space station crashed in Berlin due to unstable conditions in its orbit after exiting a time warp over the city. Evidence of the space station is said to be scattered around the city of Berlin, including another distinctive Berlin landmark, the Berliner Fernsehturm (or Berlin Television Tower). The large broadcast tower with a mirrored ball on the top is rumored to be the space station's antennae, uncovered by East German scientists.

HACKERS TO MAKERS

The maker movement got its name from *Make:* magazine, a publication dedicated to DIY projects involving computers, robots, electronics, 3D printing, metalworking, woodworking, and CNC routing. The magazine was first published in 2005, and a year later it launched the first Maker Faire, a public event celebrating "arts, crafts,

A student in Reston, Virginia, works to assemble a prosthetic hand for a disabled veteran during a Make-a-Thon.

engineering, science projects and the DIY mindset," according to the group's website. A key characteristic of the maker movement is an emphasis on community building and sharing ideas, bringing people together for not only DIY but DIWO (do it with others) creative projects. Today, there are more than 240 Maker Faires happening annually around the world.

At the same time, the Massachusetts Institute of Technology (MIT) created its Fab Lab, a small-scale workshop dedicated to digital fabrication within the famous MIT Media Lab. MIT professor Neil Gershenfeld and his colleagues started the Fab Lab to create, in their own words, "a technical prototyping platform for innovation and invention, providing stimulus for local entrepreneurship. It is also a platform for learning and innovation: a place to play, to create, to learn, to mentor, to invent."

Fab Labs typically contain digital equipment and tools to help in designing and fabricating products. They are designed as places where people can come together, exchange ideas, collaborate, and create physical objects— often with digital tools. Like hackerspaces, they foster an environment of information sharing and collaboration.

Fab Labs and digital media labs are now appearing in other educational and library spaces. Many schools are introducing makerspaces as part of their curricula, repurposing shop classes and creating dedicated spaces in the library to encourage engagement with science, engineering, and fabrication. Makerspaces provide needed space for students to create, build, invent, and tinker—and get valuable STEM (science, technology, engineering, and mathematics) experience and knowledge in the process.

CHAPTER TWO

CAREER OPTIONS: DESIGN

It's a saying among designers that the best designs are the ones that users don't really have to think about. So you may not even be aware that you interact with design pretty much all the time. That coffee cup you're drinking out of? The chair you sit in, that's just the right height for your desk? The "desktop" image on your computer that you interface with every day? The "like" button on your social media? The menu you scroll through when you save a movie to your queue? The graphics that tell you which movie to watch? Those are all created by designers.

Industrial designers create your furniture. Digital, broadcast, and graphic designers create visual communications for all kinds of media, including entertainment, advertising, print publications, games, television, web browsers, even the icons and apps on your phone. All of those people have training and experience in creating exactly the kind of design that will solve a problem or communicate a vision in

Designers create your furniture, your web page interface, and even the book you're reading right now. They think about how to make things usable.

their field, whether it's through a wireframe, an architectural plan, a game design, or a movie poster. They make sure that your coffee cup doesn't burn your hand. They also use typography to let you know that the movie you're going to see is a horror movie and not a romantic comedy.

These different types of design—traditional graphic design, industrial design, game design, interior design, user experience design, and typography—all have one thing in common, which is they solve a problem and communicate a vision. Designers create something that wasn't there before. They make something that's intended for a user to use.

Traditional design fields, like graphic design, industrial design, and game design, may be taught in school, but they often don't require a degree or license. User interaction (UI) and user experience (UX) are newer areas of interactive design that have come about in the digital age, and they also have their own traditions of design thinking. But they, too, often don't require much in the way of professional credentials beyond experience. In fact, interactive UI and UX design are not often taught in traditional design programs, which focus more on traditional graphic design and art instruction. As the technology field grows and develops in complexity, designers will be needed who can apply design principles to newer disciplines, as well.

So how do you build the skills for a career as a designer? If you guessed makerspaces and hackerspaces, you'd be right. Let's take a look at the role of designers in industry, technology, and games, and the most common routes people can take to become professional designers.

INTERACTIVE DESIGN

What do we mean when we talk about "interactive design"? The *Encyclopedia of Human-Computer Interaction* says interactive design is all "about shaping digital things for people's use." It's a discipline that encompasses all that implies about the way we use digital objects and how human cognition, emotion, and behavior play a part in how

Designers must consider everything involved in the interaction—the device, the environment, and how the device fits in your hand—to create a great user experience.

we interact with them. In short, it's about what makes digital things usable.

When you design digital things for human use, you take into account an interconnected system of everything involved in the interaction—the device, the interface, the context, the environment, and the people—in its entirety. For instance, if you create a fantastic phone with a great user interface, but it's too big for people to hold comfortably in their hand, or the screen is too dark to see at night, that's a problem with the interactive design. Interactive designers sometimes call these "friction points"—points at which users experience a less-than-smooth interaction and are taken outside of the experience. Solving these kinds of problems is what makes design so fascinating.

BASIC PRINCIPLES OF INTERACTIVE DESIGN

There's an entire discipline of design that is used to develop usable interactivity, whether it's for an application, a phone menu, a game, or a website. Over the years, a few basic principles of interactive design have been developed, which most professional interactive designers agree are the touchstones of what makes a well-designed interaction.

- Match user experience with expectations: If users are expecting a certain layout of information, sequence of steps, and terminology, matching their prior experience will cut down on the friction and discomfort of learning a new system. For this reason, it's good to know the common conventions and UI patterns used by most of the industry.

- Consistency: Similarly, you want to remain consistent throughout the entire user experience of your interface or site in interaction, layout, and consistency. For instance, if you have an Exit button in the upper right-hand corner of a page, and then suddenly on another page it says Escape and it's in the lower left-hand corner, that's an inconsistent design.
- Cognitive load: This is a concept related to the above; in designing interactions, designers need to take into account the amount of "thinking work" that it takes for the user to complete a task. One good way to reduce cognitive load on the user is to allow the computer to take on part of that load—essentially, let the computer do the thinking when it comes to that task. If the computer makes it easier for the user to do what he or she wants, that's usually because it's reduced the cognitive load of doing the task.

- Engagement: In his book *Flow: The Psychology of Optimal Experience*, Mihaly Csikszentmihalyi describes an optimal user

A fun game is one in which the interface doesn't cause friction and users feel like they can explore and get lost in the game.

experience in which people are so engaged in an activity that they lose track of the rest of the world. They are engaged in a flow experience. "Flow" has become a byword for what the designer desires to achieve through engaging interactions. Ideally, the user will be able to concentrate on what he or she wants to achieve, not on how to interact with the user interface. When the user is jarred out of the interactive experience—either by frustration or by having to think too hard about what happens next—this interrupts flow.

- Control, trust, and explorability: The user needs to trust that the system will protect him or her from making irrecoverable errors and that he or she is in control of the system at all times. If a user feels like his or her work might be lost or it's too easy to make a stupid mistake, trust is lost. If the user feels confident that he or she can use the system well, the user will feel free to explore further.

So as you can see, a designer's job is not just to make things prettier or add bells and whistles. There's an entire discipline of design that is used to develop usable interactivity, whether it's for an application, a phone menu, a game, or a website.

JOBS IN INTERACTIVE DESIGN

What kind of jobs can you get in interactive design, and who is hiring interactive designers? Many of the higher-paid jobs are in advertising and digital agencies. An agency is a group of creative professionals who bring their expertise to clients, whether it's an advertising campaign or a complete website solution. Interactive designers can also work as part of an in-house team at software companies or as part of a product UX or UI department.

According to Glassdoor, interactive designers can make from $58,317 a year for a designer to $92,557 a year for a user experience designer. Senior interactive designer positions or similar positions in places like San Francisco and New York tend to pay even more to attract top candidates.

If you work as an interactive designer, you can expect to be working as part of a team. A large part of your job will be prototyping and testing interactive solutions and communicating your vision for that solution to your colleagues and clients. You'll be coming up with different creative solutions for different clients, depending on their needs. You'll probably also be testing solutions with consumers and customers and working with their feedback to create new versions, or iterations, on your product design. So if you like a variety of creative challenges, working in a highly collaborative atmosphere, and doing a lot of A/B testing, a career in interactive design might be for you.

The need for interactive designers is not going away anytime soon. Since tools and methodology are evolving quickly, designers will be needed not just for traditional web design and interface design but for creative challenges in interaction that go beyond screens entirely. Voice activated devices and the IoT will change the way people interact in digital spaces in a way that goes beyond traditional visual design. Designers might not need the types of skills we think of as visual design skills to solve these problems, but the same principles of interactivity—thinking about what makes a digital interface work for humans—will be needed. It's a fascinating challenge that will continue to evolve in new ways in the future.

INDUSTRIAL DESIGN

Industrial designers are a lot like interactive designers, in that they create objects for humans to use. But what they create does not live only in the digital realm. It's something that exists in the real world. Furniture, household tools and appliances, consumer electronics, even automobiles and whole prefabricated houses fall into the realm of industrial design. Industrial designers must consider the usability and ergonomics of the items they produce and work to improve the function, design, and aesthetics

of that item. When coming up with an idea, the designers may visualize and sketch several different design options. For instance, when making a chair, does the chair have

These industrial designers collaborate, using CAD software to design a race car. Designers must consider how an item looks and how it will function.

armrests? A headrest? Is it cushioned or not? Made of one piece or several different interlocking pieces? How would those pieces fit together? How would they be cut out of the material being used? What height should the seat be from the floor for a human to comfortably sit in the chair? After deciding on these elements of the design, the designer will create computer renderings using computer-aided design (CAD) programs, graphic design programs, or other imaging software to create a 3D visualization of his or her design. He or she may create a 3D wireframe that will be directly used by a computer to cut out or print his or her design, using a CNC router or 3D printer.

Today, almost anyone can pick up the basic skills of industrial design by using a Fab Lab or makerspace. Smaller manufacturing puts the means to learn the basics of the design process, as well as the software and terminology, within your grasp.

JOBS IN INDUSTRIAL DESIGN

Industrial design is a highly collaborative and technical field that requires working with many different specialists, including material scientists, engineers, product planners, market researchers, and other technical and market-driven professionals to create mass-produced objects for a large number of people. The Bureau of Labor Statistics places the median annual wage for industrial designers at around $66,000. Although industrial designers work primarily in offices, they may travel to testing facilities, design centers, clients' exhibit sites, users' homes or workplaces, and places where the product is manufactured.

Most professional industrial designers have a degree in industrial design, engineering, or even architecture. But basic industrial design skills are a combination of art and engineering: drawing skills, technical knowledge, and of course, creativity, are all critical. Successful designers can combine art and engineering knowledge to create a design that's functional, sustainable, and beautiful.

As the digital world and the world of objects combine and the IoT becomes a reality, the skills involved in industrial design and interactive media design will see some overlap, especially in the world of 3D visualization. If you can gain skills in 3D wireframe and visualization software like Autocad, that can come in handy in a number of fields.

GRAPHIC DESIGN

Whether you call it graphic design, communication design, or visual branding, the term "graphic design" is used to describe a set of skills in creating visual communication, using a full set of visual tools like typography, graphics, images, symbols, layout, and composition to communicate a message. Traditional uses of graphic design include logos, magazine editorial design, advertising, web design, product packaging design, and signage. Often, a graphic designer will create a consistent "look" across all of these for a single brand or product.

A graphic design project could involve stylizing the presentation of existing text and imagery, or the creation of new text and imagery. It may incorporate either traditional print media or digital elements, photography or illustration, or even animation in the case of motion graphics.

Today, "graphic design" is an umbrella term that also encompasses the digital world of visual design, such as web design, interactive menu design, motion graphics, interface and multimedia design, animation, and icon design. Even 3D environmental design and character design for games might be considered graphic design, since they involve communicating a visual style that's in keeping with a larger brand. But for our purposes here, we will confine our discussion to the use of graphic elements to create a design, and how that relates to interactive media.

WEB DESIGN

When we talk about graphic design for interactive media, web design is what most people think of first. Web design is the process of creating a complete website, including web-page layout and design, content production, architecture, and navigation. This may sound complicated, but in reality, all these things are interconnected. You interact with them every day on the web without thinking about it—and you probably already have some instincts about what "good" or "bad" navigation feels like.

Websites are created in a markup language called hypertext markup language (HTML). Most websites define styles, layout, and aspects of appearance like fonts and

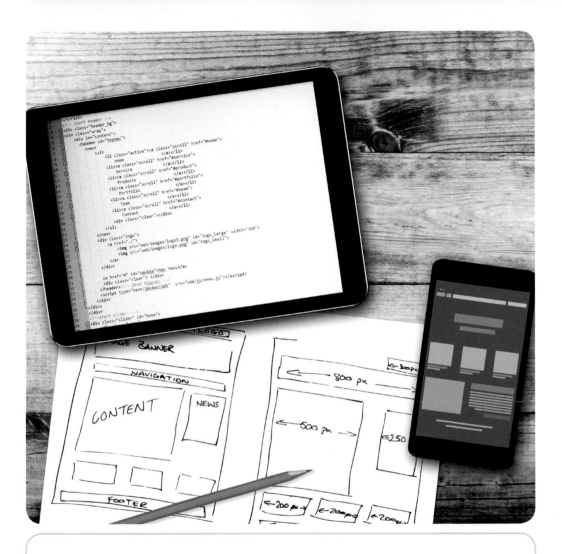

Web designers use hypertext markup language (HTML) to define layout, color, and fonts for websites.

color, through something called Cascading Style Sheets, or CSS. Designers can "hand code" pages from scratch in HTML or CSS or use an editor like Adobe Dreamweaver, often called a WYSIWYG (what you see is what you get) editor, which allows a website designer to visually manipulate the look and feel of a website or template without having to use the code.

Another popular way to create websites is through a content management system (CMS) such as Wordpress, Wix.com, or Squarespace. These services generally provide a selection of templates with varying levels of customization, which web designers can use to create websites and add content.

NAVIGATION DESIGN

There are more than 5.5 million apps available in the Apple and Android app stores, and each one of those has its own menu system and navigation design built right into it. Whether it's a drop-down menu, tabs, or what's called a breadcrumb menu, somebody gave some thought to how the user flow worked and how to navigate that app. That person is a menu designer or navigation designer.

If you've ever watched a movie on Netflix, Hulu, or Amazon Prime, you know that how you scroll through a queue, search for a movie, or go back to find your place in a season or series can vary widely between applications. Navigation is an important part of interactive design.

MOTION GRAPHICS

Motion graphics is a subset of the graphic design field that deals with animated text and graphics in a video or film production. Title sequences for movies, television shows, and news programs often make liberal use of motion graphics to set the tone, grab attention, and make introductions more entertaining. Motion graphics can use photography, typography, video, and 3D and 2D animation.

Animated infographics are also motion graphics. If you want to see the full gamut of motion graphics on display, watch the Weather Channel. You'll see moving weather maps, animated rain in a calendar, a 3D spinning station identification, and a fast-paced, bold title sequence describing a weather front—such as HURRICANE WATCH 2018—all within the space of half an hour!

A motion graphics designer is the person who creates motion graphics for a TV station or production company. He or she may be a graphic designer who has learned to integrate animation and music or may come from a background in video production. But the motion graphics designer has an eye for design and also a grasp of the software that's used to make motion graphics.

Adobe After Effects, Cinema 4D, Maya, and Blackmagic Fusion are all motion graphics software packages that are used by professionals to create custom 3D animations. While a motion graphics workspace can be intimidating to look at, the software is accessible and may even be part of your school's digital media lab. If you have the Adobe Creative Suite, After Effects is part of that package and can be picked up by anyone who knows Photoshop.

HOW MAKERSPACES AND HACKERSPACES CAN LAUNCH YOUR DESIGN CAREER

If you have a makerspace or hackerspace at your school, that's the best place to start asking questions and exploring the software that you use to create designs. Find out what's at your school or local makerspace, and if there's a design package that you particularly want, ask for it. Your school may not be able to afford a Maya license, for example, but it may find another 3D wireframe tool that will help you get the skills you need and start creating a design portfolio. Or your school may surprise you and find the budget for what you need—just because you asked.

Remember, sharing resources and using the DIY ethic is the backbone of makerspace and hackerspace culture. Being a part of it means contributing with your creativity and participation, which makes a better makerspace for everybody.

MAKERSPACES FOSTER DESIGN THINKING

Interactive technology is a central part of life today, in our everyday communication, our entertainment, and even our education. We access information, digital media, and sometimes even go to school or our jobs through digital interactions. For this reason, we need to become literate, not just in a conventional book-reading sense, but in the interactive media that surrounds us every day and that will be even more commonplace tomorrow.

An environment that actively engages students in their own learning, encouraging them to think critically, solve problems creatively, and work in a team environment prepares them to solve problems like a designer would. Makerspaces and hackerspaces provide such an environment, where students can fire up their imaginations and utilize their critical problem-solving skills. By engaging in hands-on activities, like building objects with a 3D printer or CNC router, or programming a digital app or game, students aren't just learning hard skills (though those are nice, too). They're also learning skills like problem solving, conceptual ideation, production planning, and brainstorming. The design process requires students to think about the thinking process itself.

CHAPTER THREE

CAREER OPTIONS: CODING AND DEVELOPMENT

N ow we get into the guts of interactive development: coding. Code is what we call the actual programming language used to create digital media. Coders are the people who can write the language used by the computer to create digital, and sometimes real, objects. They're also sometimes called programmers or engineers.

The idea of learning to code can be daunting for some people, but if you pick it up, it's a highly paid skill that can be your ticket to almost any industry that uses code. It's not considered as "glamorous" as design, but it can be just as creative, sometimes more so. For instance, with a tiny programmable drive like Raspberry Pi, you can design your own robot, create a video game arcade machine, or even make a remote-controlled toy car. One young woman used Raspberry Pi to create a networked knitting machine that can "print" knitted tapestries from images, including photographs, or maps of the galaxy. The sky's the limit when you know how to code!

A Code-a-Thon is a great place to get together with others in the coding community and collaborate intensively on creative coding solutions.

ONES AND ZEROS: THE LANGUAGE OF CODE

Code is a language that computers speak. It creates the graphical user interface—or GUI—that we experience as "the web." It also can tell a 3D printer how to make a whistle or a coffeemaker when to start the coffee. But it all starts with 1s and 0s: the basic binary of code.

There are many different computer languages that you can learn to get started as a programmer: HTML, extensible

KNIT ONE, AND PURL, TOO

Sarah Spencer, a software engineer from Melbourne, Australia, liked to knit as a hobby when she got hold of a vintage 1980s Brother domestic knitting machine. The machine had an onboard scanner that allowed scanning of knitting patterns, and that gave Spencer an idea. Hacking the thirty-year-old machine, Spencer used a Raspberry Pi controller to turn it into a networked printer, basically allowing her to "print" knitted tapestries from an image.

"By using a floppy drive emulator written in Python and a web interface, I can send an image to the Raspberry

A Raspberry Pi is a tiny computer the size of a credit card, which was developed to help people learn the basics of computer science.

Pi over the network, preview it in a knitting grid, and tell it to send the knitting pattern to the knitting machine via the floppy drive port," says Spencer.

Now, she makes large knitted tapestries and sells them in her Etsy shop. She's able to do custom work from a scanned image, such as photographs and team mascots. But her most famous tapestry so far is *Stargazing*, a gigantic celestial map of the night sky, including all eighty-eight constellations in the northern and southern hemispheres, and the Milky Way. Due to memory limitations on the vintage Brother, the tapestry was knitted in over twenty-one seamless file transfers. The final product took over one hundred hours of work, and weighs about 33 pounds (15 kilograms).

markup language (XML), C++, Python, and others. While all of these are useful in different contexts, it's probably best not to get too hung up on which code to learn. First, decide what it is that you want to do. The type of code you'll want to learn will proceed from there.

If you are interested in making a web page, HTML will be a useful thing for you to know. If you want to make a game, you can start out with a simple game engine like Unity. But if you really want to get into the guts of how programming works, you can try to create your own simple computer using open-source platforms like Arduino and Raspberry Pi. You can learn the basics of creating a simple code while you're building a robot. And who doesn't want to learn how to build a robot?

Makerspaces and hackerspaces are a great place to prepare for a career as a code engineer. Read on to discover some of the things that a makerspace can help you with as you learn programming.

THE RISE OF THE ROBOTS: ARDUINO

When you are programming a computer language, you are generally programming that language for something called a "platform." For instance, all the apps in the Apple store run on the iPhone platform. If you tried to run an iPhone app on an Android phone, it simply wouldn't work, because that language doesn't work on the Android platform. That's why, when you try to play *Fortnite* against your friend with a PS4 and you have an Xbox, you can't play in the same environment. You're playing what looks like the same game, but the code has been developed for different platforms.

In makerspaces, there's a platform called Arduino that has become very popular for building simple or complex electronics projects. What we call "Arduino" consists of two parts: a physical programmable circuit board, sometimes referred to as a "microcontroller," and a piece of software called an integrated development environment (IDE) that runs on your computer. The IDE is used to write and upload computer code to the physical board.

The Arduino platform has become popular with people who are just starting to learn electronics, for a few reasons. First, it's open source, which means it's not owned by anyone, and you don't need a software license to use it. Second, it is simple, cheap, and easy to program for. Using your home or school computer, you can load new code

Programmers often work as part of a larger development team, so it's important to have good communication skills as well as coding skills.

onto the Arduino board with a common Universal Serial Bus (USB) cable. And the code used by the Arduino IDE is a highly simplified version of C++, making it easy to learn.

Unlike Raspberry Pi, Arduino is not a complete computer. It's a circuit board that has one main purpose or task: to interface with sensors and devices. That might not sound very exciting, but it has actually been used for some very sophisticated systems. One Arduino project that you can make from online instructions is an Arduino Servo Catapult, which fires off a bowl full of food when a cat walks onto a pressure mat in front of its dish. Another project lets you turn a Nerf gun into a sentry turret that can sense and track enemies. Someone even used Arduino to add a fingerprint scanner to a garage door opener. The possibilities are only limited by your imagination—and lack of processor.

RASPBERRY PI: A BITE-SIZED COMPUTER

Raspberry Pi is sometimes considered an alternative to Arduino and sometimes a complementary technology, which might seem a little confusing at first. Basically, the difference between the two is that Raspberry Pi is a full minicomputer. It has a processor, memory, and graphics driver that allows you to output visuals through a high-definition multimedia interface (HDMI) cable. You could take every game in a 1980s arcade, put it on a secure digital (SD) card or drive attached to a Raspberry Pi, and use that to play them on your TV—and some people have done that!

So Raspberry Pi is able to handle more complicated trans-actions than the Arduino. But the downside is that it's a little more complicated to program for a beginner.

Raspberry Pi kits are available online for very little cost, and that's one reason why it's become so popular with hobbyists and makers. It also runs on a simplified version of Linux, an open source computer operating system.

WORKING AS A CODER

If you like to know how things work and enjoy the process of authoring and testing software, you could do a lot worse than choosing a career as a coder. Programming is one of the highest-paying and most in-demand jobs in the market these days, with some coders drawing salaries in the six-figure range. And it does not require a four-year degree, just interest and experience.

In fact, makerspaces and hackerspaces are a perfect environment for developing your chops as a computer programmer. You can learn by doing and see if a career in software development is right for you. More than just learning programming syntax in a vacuum, makerspaces and hackerspaces allow you to put your skills into the context of actual development. You'll learn to collaborate with teams, ask the right questions, and learn some solid principles and standard processes of testing, deploying, and debugging software. Anyone can learn to code—but knowing the standard procedures to report a bug and fix it will give you a big leg up over someone who just knows how to code in C++.

WHO EMPLOYS CODERS?

These days, nearly every company of any size needs a dedicated team to provide software solutions at some level. Web development teams, game companies, software companies, and even government agencies and airports are creating software for their internal and external purposes. Coders can develop something as small as an app for a phone or something as big as tracking software for the National Aeronautics and Space Administration (NASA). Each is its own challenge, and the field is constantly changing and growing. Some careers will require background checks; for example, creating a secure software solution for a government agency. But most do not require a college degree if you know the code they're looking for.

Recently, the Bureau of Labor Statistics reported that programmers made an average annual salary of around $82,000. Starting salaries are probably lower, but it's not uncommon for experienced coders to make six-figure salaries, and many even work from home.

WHAT IS THE WORK LIKE?

It's a common stereotype that programmers are better at dealing with computers than people. But the truth is, successful programmers need to have people skills, too. A good developer not only has the ability to write clean code but can communicate well with teams and translate business requirements into elegant technical solutions. Even if you are working remotely (and in a large

Programmers often work as part of a larger development team, so it's important to have good communication skills as well as coding skills.

programming team, a common practice), you need to be able to work well with others. In fact, communication is even more critical for remote teams.

The work itself requires a lot of iteration and testing. Author, compile, test, deploy, debug: these are the steps of software iteration. It takes patience, attention to detail, and an understanding of scientific method. If you are the type of person who likes to fly by the seat of your pants and worry about details later—maybe software development isn't for you!

One challenge in this area is to keep up your skills. New languages are always being developed, and it's important to stay abreast of new developments in code so your skills remain relevant.

Makerspaces and hackerspaces are a great place to test both your interest and aptitude in coding, in an environment where you can explore and ask questions. The best approach is to come to the makerspace with a specific project in mind. Start simple, and concentrate on learning how code works. Once you pick up the basics of coding and iterating in one programming language, those skills will translate to whatever programming challenges you want to work on next.

CHAPTER FOUR

GAME DESIGN

Now that we've got a handle on the basic principles of design and coding, you're prepared to learn about a form of interactive media where these two fields come together: video game design.

You may think that being a game designer means you get to play games all day, but game design is a very specific discipline. It requires learning a set of tools, collaborating with other designers, artists and programmers, and iterating on a design together many times to create the "fun." Sometimes you can work on a game for years and years before it's ready to be played. But if you love working long hours on a creative solution and iterating on a design with teams—and yes, playing that same game over and over— then you probably will like working in the game industry.

A lot of people aspire to make video games, but that doesn't mean it's impossible to break into this competitive field. Many game designers start their careers as independent developers, tinkering with the tools and getting familiar with the game development environment until they're able to create the game they envision. In fact, many game development companies now look for candidates who have created a game, or are at least familiar with the basic

The video games you enjoy took years, a lot of work, and a lot of people to create.

principles of building a simple game in a widely available game engine. The accessibility of robust game engines has made this possible.

If you don't have the tools to create games at home, a makerspace or hackerspace is a great place to get started with some hands-on experience in a game development environment. You're also likely to find like-minded collaborators who can help you on your journey to designing the games of your dreams.

START YOUR ENGINES!

Remember when we talked about an integrated development environment (IDE)? Well, the IDE for creating games is called a game engine. Developers use different game engines to create games for consoles, computers, and mobile phones. A game engine generally has a set of visual development tools and software components that allow you to do the different things you need to create the game in a seamless environment. A graphics renderer (2D or 3D) creates your visual assets, like environments and characters. Artificial intelligence (AI) allows you to give your nonplayable characters, or NPCs, something to do. Physics and collision detection mean your game world behaves like a real world, and you don't just fall through floors or find things floating in midair. You'll also usually find ways to add audio and animation, textures and lighting, memory management, threading, and what's called "localization" support (which allows any text in the game to be ported to another language).

Did you know there was so much going on in the background of your first-person shooter? Let's take a look under the hood and examine some of the more popular game engines on the market.

UNITY

Unity is a popular game engine for independent developers, for many reasons. First, it allows you to create impressive 2D and 3D games for very little money. There is a free version of the software that you can download and use for personal use, so it's easy to get started poking around in Unity. Finally, you can port to almost any platform from Unity, so you can create versions of your game for mobile, desktop, and even Xbox, PlayStation, and Nintendo. Although if you are serious about porting your game to different platforms for commercial use, you'll probably have to pay

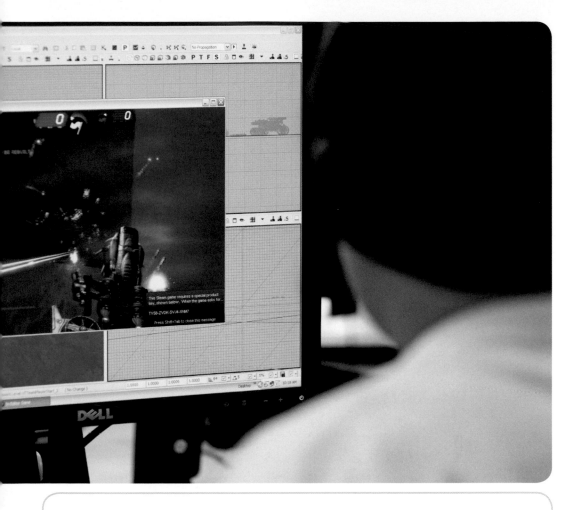

The Unreal engine is a popular game development tool. Here, an iD Tech Camp participant plays through a scene he created in Unreal 3.5.

for a license to the pro version of Unity, which can be a little pricey.

For a first-time game designer, Unity might be a little complex. But the coding language itself is pretty accessible for beginners, in that it resembles HTML and XML. It's worth downloading and taking a look around just to see what's available and what you're able to do.

UNREAL

Unreal is a game engine that was developed by Epic Games back in the 1990s. Now in its fourth version, it has lasted so long because it's a very flexible and extensible tool set, that allows game designers to create complete worlds within its development environment, including lighting, textures, and a level editor that lets mappers design level layouts on the fly.

Over the years, Unreal has become the industry standard for many of the larger game companies and has built up a base of code that has been extended, refined, and improved through many generations of games, from *Duke Nukem* and *Deus Ex* to *Fortnite*.

In Unreal 4, there is a free version of the engine that anyone can use, and many Unreal developer communities also have libraries of Unreal assets that you can use to create games—characters, buildings, and animations that other people have created in Unreal that you can "plug and play" into your own Unreal games.

In 2018, Epic Games announced a new learning platform for Unreal, the Unreal Engine Online Learning Site, which hosts online training and video tutorials to walk learners through all the common Unreal work flows. To download the free engine and start learning, visit the Unreal Engine website.

NEVERWINTER NIGHTS: CHOOSE YOUR OWN PATH

If you are more interested in the narrative side of game development, you've probably heard of BioWare. Its games are famous for richly interactive storytelling and include titles like *Mass Effect*, *Dragon Age*, and *Star Wars: The Old Republic*.

BioWare has a simple test for its aspiring narrative designers: download the Neverwinter Nights engine (an early engine that it used for the game *Neverwinter Nights*) and construct a game module with branching choices. The test is simple, but not easy. It's a challenge to learn the mechanics of a new game engine, but by learning the tools of the trade, you can assure the design-

BioWare developed the *Mass Effect* series, which is famous for its sophisticated and engaging interactive storytelling.

(*continued on the next page*)

(*continued from the previous page*)

ers at BioWare that you'll be able to jump in with your storytelling chops and start contributing to the narrative from day one.

If you want to give it a try, the engine is download-able from the BioWare site. There are many online resources for getting up to speed on the Neverwinter Nights engine. A fun challenge would be to trade mod-ules with your peers and play each other's adventures!

THE DISCIPLINE OF GAME DESIGN

Learning video game design isn't just about playing a lot of games and then mastering the game engine. Like other forms of design, there is a world of game theory and game systems design to learn if you want to make games that are fun and engaging to play. Here are a few aspects of the design disci-pline that professional game designers wrestle with:

- **Systems design and balancing.** Whether you're playing a candy crushing game on Facebook or racing in a *Mario Kart* game, part of the fun of playing a game is developing strategy and out-smarting the game. The strategy is usually based on making choices. With a limited number of turns, you choose your moves carefully. Or if you use all your energy points to plant crops, you'll need to buy more energy to build a barn.

  For instance, let's say you were playing a card strategy game against an opponent, and you were on the verge of winning the round when, suddenly, your opponent plays a card called Apocalypse that destroys all your progress and resets the board. Would you think that game was fun? Or would you "rage quit" and never want to play that game again?

The issue here is game balance. A game that is poorly balanced will cause frustration. Whether the balance is determined by limited resources (a time clock, an energy bank) or a balanced deck of cards, each game design must find its unique balance between feeling "too easy" or "too hard." That balance point is where we find something elusive, called "fun." Believe it or not, a lot of math goes into finding that balance. And it's a big part of why each game takes time to develop, since each change to the design requires the game to be rebalanced.

- **Engagement and reward.** What motivates a player to keep playing a game? Sometimes this is called "maximizing player engagement," but it's really about behavioral science. Like a rat getting a pellet, you want the player to keep pushing that button. Systems of engagement and reward are a sneaky way to make the player keep doing that. Sometimes these are called "breadcrumbs"—if you keep playing long enough, you'll unlock achievements, special boosts, or weapons, for example.
- **Quest design.** Does your game have a story? Narrative design and quests are a discipline within game design that make story-driven games feel like a movie that stars you (or you, playing a character).

Understanding how to write for games is different from writing for a traditional narrative. You need to center the player in a story and create compelling drama around that.

HOW TO PREPARE FOR THIS CAREER

According to the Gamasutra Game Developers Salary survey of 2014, game developers in the United States averaged about $83,060 in salaries that year, down 2 percent from 2013. At major game companies, these salaries have stayed about the same, though smaller companies may pay less (especially at the beginner level).

The best way to prepare to be a game designer is to

download a game engine and design a game module. With the number of open source game engines available

Level design, environment design, and narrative design are all aspects of game design, and you can learn a lot by developing your own modules with open source software.

online, this is something many companies are starting to require from anyone applying as a designer. There are other specializations within game design that you might want to look at as well, if it's a better fit for your skills and interests. Environment artists, character artists, and animators are all creative professionals who help bring a game to life.

Another great way to break in is the classic n00b (newbie) job: quality assurance, or QA. Otherwise known as "game testing," this is a great place to get a feel for the game company of your dreams and get a foot in the door, even with no experience. You'll work long hours, but you'll prove yourself as a part of the team and learn as you go.

CHAPTER FIVE

DIGITAL MEDIA

Today, people are shooting broadcast-quality video with phones and creating their own channels on YouTube, Twitch, and streaming services. You can produce a podcast in your closet and upload it to the Apple Store. More and more, shooting, editing, color correcting, and audio production are all skills that your average YouTuber is able to achieve at a level that used to be reserved for pros. But how are they picking up those skills? And just as importantly, how can you?

Sure, you can watch a few tutorials on YouTube. But if you really want to build your skills up to a pro level, digital media labs can provide the resources, equipment, and know-how to take your videos and podcasts to the next level.

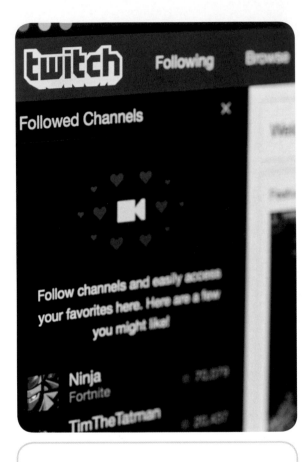

As streaming video becomes popular across platforms, viewers demand more content.

MAKERSPACES AND THE RISE OF THE DIGITAL MEDIA LAB

Digital media labs are creative spaces where you can borrow or rent low-cost equipment for your video and audio productions, such as cameras, lights, microphones, and tripods. Sometimes they will include coworking space, or computer time rentals for video and audio editing, loaded with the proper editing and color correction software, like Pro Tools, Final Cut, and Adobe Premiere and After Effects. Today's digital media labs may even include sophisticated production setups like a green screen (used for chroma keying), a soundproof audio studio, or even facilities for creating still-frame or stop-motion animation.

Audiovisual labs, or clubs, have been parts of school and public libraries for many years. The digital media lab at your public library probably started as a place to convert analog to digital media. But over time, this kind of media

AUSTIN CINEMAKER SPACE

Founded in 2016 in a repurposed industrial warehouse in East Austin, Texas, Austin Cinemaker Space grew out of the community-oriented Austin School of Film and its sister space, the Motion Media Arts Center. It fills a need for an affordable creative coworking space and makerspace for the Austin creative community, with access to state-of-the-art technology, studio space, and youth programs.

Austin Cinemaker Space is Austin's only nonprofit coworking membership and makerspace program for digital media. It rents equipment, provides studio rentals and production space, hosts cast and crew calls, and has an iMac lab that members can use to cut their projects in-house. It also has an extensive learning program, offering workshops and even certification programs for video and audio professionals.

The space is the brainchild of Faiza Kracheni, education and programming director of the Austin School of Film. While programming classes for Austin School of Film in 2014, Kracheni took a trip to Brooklyn, where she visited a video production coworking space that was in a section of Vice headquarters. "It was very industrial and minimal," says Kracheni. "It worked well for filmmakers and media artists who need multi-use space for day to day needs." She realized that her organization could offer something similar to the filmmaking community through a low-cost membership program.

Cinemaker Space took the makerspace model to cinema and became a place where Austin visual and

(*continued on the next page*)

(*continued from the previous page*)

> video artists can meet, share ideas, and have access to resources.
>
> "I thought it was important for the community to have a low-cost alternative to education, workspace, and tools," says Kracheni. "Socioeconomic or cultural backgrounds should never stunt access, and this is why we exist."

digitization has developed into a bigger focus on full-fledged production. In this, these labs took a page from the makerspace book and became a place where creative individuals could learn, help each other, pool resources, and rent equipment. A digital media lab typically also includes an educational component in the form of workshops, professional speakers, or equipment training.

If you are working on a creative project and need to use digital video or audio equipment, find collaborators, or rent a space to host your script reading or shoot against a green screen, you can get you what you need from a digital media lab without investing hundreds or thousands of dollars.

WHO EMPLOYS VIDEO AND AUDIO PROS?

As digital video continues to dominate social media channels, demand for compelling content skyrockets—and with that demand, an opportunity for people who want to create video content.

Digital media labs are a great way to access tools and develop the skills to create professional-looking video.

According to industry research firm Business Insider Intelligence, digital video advertisement revenue is projected to rise at a rate of 21.9 percent annually through 2020. And that means large and small companies are looking at ways to get into those channels. Almost every company is looking for a way to market on Facebook, Instagram, and YouTube, which get billions of views a day.

CHAPTER SIX

NEXT GEN TECH: THE FUTURE OF INTERACTIVE MEDIA

C areers in digital media are only going to continue to expand in the future, and the best place to get hands-on experience in the latest technology are places like makerspaces, hackerspaces, and digital media labs. Working together, a group of enthusiasts will often have resources and knowledge that even college-level classes do not. And the flexibility of a makerspace and hackerspace allows the group to pursue, and respond to, exciting new developments in the ever-evolving world of digital media.

It's almost impossible to predict which way interactive media will head in the future. But here are just a few of the new areas of development that media creators, designers, and programmers are excited about.

Virtual reality, or VR, is another platform for developing immersive games and 3D content.

VIRTUAL REALITY

When you put on a VR headset, virtual reality technology puts you into a computer-generated environment that's completely immersive and 3D. Eye and head tracking, a mobile sensor or gyroscope, and magnetic sensors to identify the person's position relative to the ground help complete the virtual reality illusion.

Today, VR headsets like Oculus Rift have become a new platform for games and other forms of immersive entertainment, such as *EVE: Valkyrie*, a first-person fighter pilot game that takes advantage of VR technology to create excitement, immersion, and even vertigo. Other, less stomach-churning applications for the technology are also being considered, such as virtual home tours for realtors, simulations for training exercises (for actual pilots), and even doctor's visits.

AUGMENTED REALITY

Virtual reality's cousin is augmented reality (AR)—a technology that superimposes computer-generated images on top of a user's view of the real world, in a composite of computer imagery and reality.

With mobile games like *Pokémon Go* or the Harry Potter AR game, *Wizards Unite*, augmented reality has already become a familiar part of our everyday life and play. But people are finding other creative uses of AR, as well. One company has found a use for it as augmented art: wave your phone over a comic book, cover, for example, and you can see the art animate.

Research continues to bring the future of AR beyond phones and tablets. Google Glass, the wearable AR goggles, may have gotten shelved due to unpopularity, but other wearable devices, including AR functionality in contact lenses, are in development, as well as new ways of thinking about how VR and AR can exist in the world.

COMICS ARE ALIVE: A THOUGHT BUBBLE ART TRAIL

Artist and comic creator Sutu, aka Stu Campbell, hopes you will explore the world through art. He and his business partner Lukasz Karluk have developed an app called EyeJack, an augmented reality phone app and platform that uses AR as a tool for storytelling and artistic expression. At a recent comic book convention, Thought Bubble 2018, they created an art trail of augmented reality throughout the convention. Called Comics Are Alive, visitors were encouraged to find the fifteen pieces of augmented art throughout the convention by using the EyeJack app.

"At the moment it's a strange experience to wave your phone over a book to see animated content," Sutu says. But augmenting the printed artwork with an animation—or in some cases, augmenting a blank wall with some animated digital graffiti—allows a new layer of artistic meaning to emerge.

"I encouraged the artists to explore the possibilities of AR art in their own style," says Sutu. "The result is a diverse collection of AR art ranging from hand drawn illustrations to technical 3-D animations to powerful political narrative, all of which beautifully showcases the potential of the medium."

Holograms are another application of VR that researchers are exploring. Since holograms can be seen and heard by a group of people, and not just an individual, it's a way of thinking about virtual reality that takes it out of the realm of isolated, individual experience and into the world.

INTERACTIVE STORYTELLING

Recently, the streaming giant Netflix announced that it was planning a slate of interactive TV shows, starting with an episode of the popular dystopian science-fiction series *Black Mirror*. Netflix had floated the concept in some of its original children's programming, like *Puss in Boots*, but it is now negotiating deals for other live-action TV shows aimed at adults.

Carla Engelbrecht Fisher, director of

product innovation at Netflix, has gone on record to say that the children's programming space was a "natural place" to start with interactive programming, "since kids are

Black Mirror is a popular science-fiction show on Netflix. New seasons always draw a large audience of viewers.

eager to 'play' with their favorite characters and already inclined to tap, touch and swipe at screens. They also talk to their screens, as though the characters can hear them. Now, that conversation can be two way. It's really about finding the right stories—and storytellers—that can tell these complex narratives and bring them to life in a compelling way."

Will the final entertainment platform be our own brain? One thing's for sure: the future of interactive media is a trip.

GLOSSARY

A/B testing In market research, A/B testing is the process of showing two different versions of a website or product to potential consumers and seeing which one they like better.

Arduino An open source, programmable circuit board that can be integrated into a variety of maker projects, both complex and simple.

assets In game design, game assets are any elements or objects that can be used within the game engine, including 3D models (characters, environments, objects, vehicles), code snippets, modules, music, and sound effects.

collision detection The computational problem of detecting how two or more objects will intersect or collide in physical simulations and vide games.

content management system (CMS) A software application or interface that allows a user to create and manage digital content without having to edit code.

ergonomics The study of how to arrange workspaces, products, or furniture so that they fit the people who use them.

hacker A skilled computer programmer who uses technical knowledge to solve a problem.

integrated development environment (IDE) An application that coders work within to develop further applications.

interface In computing, any shared boundary between which components of a computer system exchange information.

IoT (internet of things) The network of physical devices embedded with electronics, software, sensors, and internet connections that can connect, collect, and exchange data (includes vehicles, home appliances, and home security systems).

iteration A sequence of actions done over and over again to get closer to a desired result.

microcontroller A small computer that contains one or more CPUs (processor cores), memory, and programmable input/output peripherals.

open source Software for which the original source code is made freely available to the public and can be redistributed and modified without a software license.

platform A particular environment that software runs on.

prototyping Creating a first preliminary iteration of something, especially a machine, which serves as the model from which other forms are developed or copied.

Raspberry Pi A simple, credit-card-sized computer with a single circuit board, developed by the Raspberry Pi Foundation to promote the teaching of computer science.

STEM (science, technology, engineering, and math) As developed in 2009, STEM refers to a course of interdisciplinary learning in which students learn science, technology, engineering, and math by using applied science concepts in a hands-on context, preparing them for technology jobs in the future.

virtual reality A 3D simulation, generated by computer, that creates an environment that can be interacted with in a seemingly real or physical way.

WYSIWYG editor Stands for "what you see is what you get." Allows content to be edited without using code.

FOR MORE INFORMATION

Austin Cinemaker Space
2200 Tillery Street
Austin, TX 78723
(512) 236-8877
Website: https://www.austinfilmschool.org
Facebook: @AustinSchoolofFilm
Instagram: @austinschooloffilm
Austin Cinemaker Space is a coworking space and maker-
space for filmmakers and creatives. It is affiliated with
Austin Film School and open to the public.

Autodesk Technology Center at Pier 9
Pier 9, 9 The Embarcadero
San Francisco, CA 94111
(415) 356-0700
Website: https://www.autodesk.com
Facebook, Instagram, and Twitter: @autodesk
Pier 9 is a hub for research and development of new manu-
facturing technologies. Autodesk, the publisher of CAD,
a leading 3D visualization software, hosts symposiums
and demonstrations at Pier 9.

C-Base, Berlin
Rungestraße 20, 10179
Berlin, Germany
+49 30 28599300
Website: https://www.c-base.org
Twitter: @cbase
One of the earliest hackerspaces, C-Base in Berlin is host

to the Chaos Computer Club, the Berlin Wikipedia editors group, and several other hacker societies.

Gamasutra
303 Second Street, 9th Floor
San Francisco, CA 94107
(415) 947-6000
Website: http://www.gamasutra.com
Facebook: @Gamasutra
Twitter: @gamasutra
Gamasutra is the leading website covering the game industry, news, and technology.

Hybrid Lab at CCA
California College of the Arts
1111 Eighth Street
San Francisco, CA 94107-2247
(800) 447-1ART (1278)
Website: https://www.cca.edu/hybrid-lab
Facebook: @CaliforniaCollegeoftheArts
Instagram: @cacollegeofarts
Twitter: @CACollegeofArts
The CCA Hybrid Lab is a leading Silicon Valley makerspace lab for shared interdisciplinary innovations and resources.

Make: magazine
1700 Montgomery Street, Suite 240
San Francisco, CA 94111
Website: http://www.makermedia.com
Facebook and Instagram: @makemagazine
Twitter: @make

YouTube: @makemagazine
A leading voice of the maker movement, *Make:* magazine
 publishes projects, tutorials, and other resources accessible to all ages and skill ranges.

MakerCube
5947 206a St #104B,
Langley, BC V3A 8M1
Canada
(604) 362-4291
Website: https://www.makercube.ca
Facebook: @MakerCubeCanada
Instagram: @makercube
Twitter: @MakerCube
A lab in Langley, Canada, that provides equipment in a
 collaborative coworking space.

MIT Media Lab
Massachusetts Institute of Technology
75 Amherst Street
Cambridge, MA 02139
(617) 253-5960
Website: https://www.media.mit.edu
Facebook and Instagram: @mitmedialab
Twitter: @medialab
The MIT Media Lab is an "antidisciplinary" research lab
 that encourages the mixing of disciplines such as media,
 science, art, and design.

Protospace Ltd (Calgary)
Bays 108 & 110, 1530 Twenty-Seventh Avenue NE

Calgary, AB T2E 7S6
Canada
(587) 774-5672
Website: http://www.protospace.ca
Facebook and Twitter: @protospace
Protospace is Calgary's original, community-based,
    member-driven makerspace. Protospace offers
    workshop space, shared tools, and financial aid to
    low-income members, as well as a residency program.

WIRED magazine
520 Third Street
San Francisco, CA 94107
(415) 276-5000
Website: https://www.wired.com
Facebook, Instagram, Twitter, and YouTube: @wired
WIRED is a leading publication that focuses on emerging
    technologies, particularly how they affect culture.

FOR FURTHER READING

Bailenson, Jeremy. *Experience on Demand: What Virtual Reality Is, How It Works, and What It Can Do*. New York, NY: W. W. Norton, 2018.

Banzi, Massimo, and Michael Shiloh. *Getting Started with Arduino*. Sebastapol, CA: Maker Media, 2015.

Bryan, Robert Denton, and Robert Giglio. *Slaying the Dragon: Writing Great Video Games*. Studio City, CA: Michael Weise Productions, 2016.

Ghaoui, Claude. *The Encyclopedia of Human-Computer Interaction*. Hershey, PA: Idea Group Reference, 2018.

Hand, Carol. *Getting Paid to Produce Videos*. New York, NY: Rosen Publishing, 2017.

Koster, Ralph. *A Theory of Fun for Game Design*. Scottsdale, AZ: Paraglyph Press, 2006.

Miller, Andrew. *Arduino for Beginners*. Tampa, FL: Makerspaces.com Publishing, 2018.

Richardson, Matt, and Shawn Wallace. *Getting Started with Raspberry Pi*. Sebastapol, CA: Maker Media, 2016.

Rogers, Scott. *Level Up! The Great Guide to Game Design*. Hoboken, NJ: John Wiley & Sons, 2014.

Shoftner, Melissa. *Video Game Developers: Behind the Scenes with Coders*. New York, NY: Rosen Publishing, 2018.

Althauser, Joel "Five Incredible Tools for VR Game Developers." *Orlando Business Journal*, October 22, 2018. https://www.bizjournals.com/orlando/news/2018/10/22/5-incredible-tools-for-vr-game-developers.html.

Bate, Alex. "Networked Knitting Machine: Not Your Average Knit One, Purl One." Raspberry Pi, September 25, 2018. https://www.raspberrypi.org/blog/knitting-network-printer.

Csikszentmihalyi, Mihaly. *Flow: The Psychology of Optimal Experience*. New York, NY: Harper Perennial, 2008.

Erridge, Andrew. "Building a Multiplayer RTS in Unreal Engine." Gamasutra, October 4, 2018. https://www.gamasutra.com/blogs/AndrewErridge/20181004/327885/Building_a_Multiplayer_RTS_in_Unreal_Engine.php.

Fisher, Carla Englebrecht. "Interactive Storytelling on Netflix: Choose What Happens Next." Netflix Media Center, June 20, 2017. https://media.netflix.com/en/company-blog/interactive-storytelling-on-netflix-choose-what-happens-next.

Miller, Andrew. "What Is Arduino (PDF)." Makerspaces.com. Retrieved September 17, 2018. https://www.makerspaces.com/arduino-for-beginners-book.

Miller, Liz Shannon. "The Future of Netflix Might Be Interactive TV, and It's Already Here." IndieWire, May 1, 2018. https://www.indiewire.com/2018/05/netflix-interactive-tv-stretch-armstrong-the-breakout-1201959464.

Mitra, Mikhail. "10 Basic Principles of Interaction Design." Mantra Labs Global. Retrieved September 18,

2018. https://www.mantralabsglobal.com/blogs/10-basic-principles-of-interaction-design.

New Gen Apps. "How VR Works: The Technology Behind Virtual Reality." February 9, 2018. https://www.newgenapps.com/blog/how-vr-works-technology-behind-virtual-reality.

Newton, Casey. "Netflix Interactive Shows Arrive to Put You in Charge of the Story." Verge, June 20, 2017. https://www.theverge.com/2017/6/20/15834858/netflix-interactive-shows-puss-in-boots-buddy-thunderstruck.

Olson, Todd. "So What Is Design, Anyway?" Medium, March 18, 2017. https://medium.com/the-design-innovator/https-medium-com-the-design-innovator-so-what-is-design-anyway-4f99128b51c4.

Rubin, Peter. "The *Wired* Guide to Virtual Reality." *WIRED*, September 11, 2018. https://www.wired.com/story/wired-guide-to-virtual-reality.

Starr, Michelle. "Prosthetic Reality: The Art of Augmented Reality." CNET, February 6, 2017. https://www.cnet.com/news/prosthetic-reality-the-artification-of-augmented-reality.

Stivison, Meg. "Breaking Into the Video Game Industry: Quality Assurance." August 1, 2012. https://www.animationcareerreview.com/articles/breaking-video-game-industry-quality-assurance-otherwise-known-video-game-testing.

Tweeney, Dylan. "DIYers Flock to Hackerspaces Worldwide." *WIRED*, March 29, 2009. https://www.wired.com/2009/03/hackerspaces.

Welschmeyer, Brett. "A Brief History of Makerspaces." MidMoMaker Labs, April 23, 2018. https://midmomakerlabs.com/brief-history-of-makerspaces.

INDEX

ABOUT THE AUTHOR

Janet Harvey's career in digital media began in the 1990s when, as a multimedia editor for DC Comics, she oversaw the development of *The Multipath Adventures of Superman*, a choose-your-own-path animated series that ran for six seasons on Entertaindom.com. Since then, she has been a narrative game designer for Sony Online Entertainment, Zynga, and Portalarium and designed learning-based games for several start-up e-learning companies. She also writes and directs for digital video. Her self-produced feature film, *One Million Hits*, is available on Steam.

PHOTO CREDITS

Cover (top), p. 1 Ralf Hiemisch/Getty Images; cover (bottom) Westend61/Getty Images; p. 5 Delpixel/Shutterstock.com; pp. 8–9, 52–53 Gorodenkoff/Shutterstock.com; p. 10 Agencja Fotograficzna Caro/Alamy Stock Photo; p. 12 The Washington Post/Getty Images; p. 15 Rawpixel.com/Shutterstock.com; pp. 16–17 Antonio Guillem/Shutterstock.com; p. 19 Andrey_Popov/Shutterstock.com; pp. 22–23 Monty Rakusen/Cultura/Getty Images; p. 27 ronstik/Shutterstock.com; p. 33 vgajic/E+/Getty Images; p. 34 Emma Gibbs/Moment/Getty Images; p. 37 Golubovy/Shutterstock.com; p. 41 puhhha/Shutterstock.com; pp. 44–45 adriaticfoto/Shutterstock.com; pp. 46–47 ZUMA Press Inc/Alamy Stock Photo; p. 49 Game Shots/Alamy Stock Photo; p. 56 PixieMe/Shutterstock.com; p. 59 FrameStockFootages/Shutterstock.com; p. 61 Jacob Lund/Shutterstock.com; pp. 64–65 PictureLux/The Hollywood Archive/Alamy Stock Photo; interior pages background (circuit board) Richard Newstead/ (touchscreen) Busakorn Pongparnit/Moment/Getty Images; back cover graphic Pobytov/DigitalVision Vectors/Getty Images; p. 4 illustration Bloomicon/Shutterstock.com.

Design and Layout: Michael Moy; Editor: Bethany Bryan; Photo Researcher: Karen Huang